Jules Verne

A Journey to the Centre of the Earth

CAMPFIRE™

KALYANI NAVYUG MEDIA PVT LTD
New Delhi

Sitting around the Campfire, telling the story, were:

Wordsmith	:	Lewis Helfand
Illustrator	:	Vinod Kumar
Illustrations Editor	:	Jayshree Das
Colourist	:	Ajo Kurian
Colour Consultant	:	RC Prakash
Letterer	:	Bhavnath Chaudhary
Editors	:	Suparna Deb
		Divya Dubey

Cover Artists:

Illustrator	:	Lalit Kumar
Colourist	:	Rajeev Chauhan
Designer	:	Manishi Varshney

Published by Kalyani Navyug Media Pvt Ltd
101 C, Shiv House, Hari Nagar Ashram
New Delhi 110014
India
www.campfire.co.in

ISBN: 978-81-906963-3-3

Printed in India at Rave India

About The Author

Jules Gabriel Verne was born in Nantes, France on 8th February 1828. Over the following 77 years, he became both a prodigious writer and a creator of characters that would be known throughout the world. His work continues to live on well beyond his death, and he is known by many as the father of modern science fiction.

Sent to Paris to study law, like his father before him, Verne soon discovered that his real talent lay in writing. This gift established him as an author of exciting and extravagant adventures. Sometimes, these stories revolved around the use of technologies of the day, such as in his novels *Five Days in a Balloon* and *Around the World in Eighty Days*. However, what made Verne really stand out were the flights of fancy he took with regard to the potential advances in technology. His fantastic creations were based, in many respects, on a keen understanding of science and the way it was moving forward.

In France, Verne was greatly encouraged to pursue his writing talent when he met Alexandre Dumas, the famous author. Verne produced several plays between 1851 and 1861 and, during that time, met and married Honorine Fraysse. In the years that followed, he began to concentrate on novels, and the first of his better known books was published in 1864 – *A Journey to the Centre of the Earth*.

Predicting such revolutionary concepts as gas-powered automobiles, skyscrapers, submarines, journeys to the moon and high-speed trains, Verne truly laid the groundwork for his belief that 'whatever one man is capable of conceiving, other men will be able to achieve'. He also correctly predicted that developments in technology would one day lead to the production of weapons of mass destruction.

Verne died on 24th March 1905. Whatever reasons someone has for reading his works, one thing is assured: while his stories about the future range from frighteningly accurate, to wildly speculative, his novels provide an entertaining adventure based in a world that is not that distant from our own, but is intriguing, dangerous and thrilling.

Professor Von Hardwigg

Henry

Hans Bjelke

Hamburg, Germany. 1863.

I was trying to decipher the complicated inscription on the mysterious parchment.

I studied the puzzle and tried to group the letters in every possible way. And then it came upon me like a flash of lightning. I had worked it out. To understand the document, it just needed to be read backwards.

No. No, this can't be!

How could a man possibly...

My uncle must never know about this. He would insist upon doing what it says. He is such a determined geologist that ropes could not hold him!

If he deciphers this, he will go in spite of everything, and he will take me with him, and we will never get back. Never!

I will do everything I can to prevent my uncle from discovering the contents of this document.

I was overwhelmed by horror and it took possession of my soul.

By analysing it again and again, he might discover the key. I have to destroy it.

I decided that no living being should ever know.

I was about to completely destroy this dangerous secret for good...

HENRY!

...when the study door opened, and my uncle entered. He snatched the document from my hands.

Any luck? Find out anything?

No, Uncle. Nothing.

My uncle, Professor Von Hardwigg, was a German who had married my mother's sister. As his nephew, I became his laboratory assistant.

Having found an old manuscript containing this parchment, he convinced himself it held a wonderful secret.

He was a professor of mineralogy and a learned egotist.

He laboured at the faded symbols.

I can just about make out the name. It says Arne Saknussemm.

Arne Saknussemm! That is the name of an Icelander. He was a professor from the sixteenth century, and a famous alchemist!

I will discover the secret of this document, and I will not sleep or eat until I have found it.

Nor you either, Henry!

My uncle was a well-informed man. I took a deep interest in all he did, and hoped to be as learned myself some day.

While my uncle worked on the code, my thoughts turned to Gretchen – my fiancée.

My uncle's imagination was vigorous and creative, and he would risk his life to do what other geologists had never done.

Night came and the sounds in the streets ceased. Yet, my uncle still went on, not even answering our cook when she called us for supper.

I have to tell him.

I... I made an important discovery. The coded text... it's written backwards.

Backwards! Oh, most cunning Saknussemm. I have been such a fool!

It reads, 'Descend, bold traveller, into the crater of Sneffels before the beginning of July...

...and you will reach the centre of the Earth! I did it!'

And so will I, Arne Saknussemm!

FFFRRRRR

The centre of the Earth!

On reading this my uncle jumped, as if he had received an electric shock. His joy and his conviction were magnificent to behold. He rushed about the room, wild with delight.

My uncle studied the best map on Iceland.

Here is Sneffels. It is a mountain about 5,000 feet high.

And, if its crater leads down to the centre of the Earth, it is one of the most remarkable in the world.

But that is impossible, because this crater is evidently filled with lava and burning rocks, and therefore--

It's supposedly extinct – no eruptions since 1219 – and is no longer considered an active volcano.

And so my uncle decided to set out on what seemed to be an absurd journey.

Gretchen, won't you talk me out of going?

We leave for Denmark tomorrow, my boy.

Once there, we will catch a boat to Iceland.

No, Henry. He is a bold philosopher, and a man of immense courage. He will no doubt succeed. It is admirable to devote yourself to science.

All hope was now gone. My uncle had purchased the tools and apparatus required for this desperate trip. There were rope ladders, knotted cords, torches, flasks, grappling irons, alpenstocks, pickaxes – enough for ten men!

In two days we reached Copenhagen, Denmark. A small Danish schooner, the *Valkyrie*, was to set sail for Reykjavik on 2nd June.

All the more reason why we should go up; we must get used to heights.

I will never be able to do it.

Don't be a coward; come on.

It was impossible to disagree with my uncle's logic. I gave in with a groan.

My legs gave way like those of a drunken man. I crawled on my hands and knees.

Look down! Look down well!

You must take a lesson in abysses.

The boat won't be ready for a few days. Let us walk to the top of this church.

I'll get dizzy.

Before looking down, I glanced upwards at the cold, fleecy clouds.

Tomorrow we will do it again.

And we did. For five days in succession, I was subjected to this torture. By the end of that period, I ascended happily enough, and was able to look below without even blinking, and with some degree of pleasure.

On the agreed date, we safely boarded the *Valkyrie*. It was a splendid sailer, and we were expected to reach Reykjavik in about ten days.

I dealt with the troubles of the sea pretty well. However, my uncle, to his own disgust and shame, was ill throughout the voyage.

Iceland! Mount Sneffels!

Well, Henry, we are nearly there, and the worst is now over.

The worst!

Absolutely. Now we only have to go into the bowels of the Earth.

Oh, if that is all we need to do, then you are quite right!

That is the easiest part of our business, and does not, in any way, trouble me.

But, once we have gone down, I want to know how we are to get up again.

In Reykjavik, we were received by M Fridriksson, a professor of natural science in the college of Reykjavik. He was a man of invaluable ability.

We have 8,000 volumes of the most rare and valuable works scattered all over Iceland, Professor Hardwigg.

Amongst your ancient books, do you possess any of the works of Arne Saknussemm?

You mean the sixteenth century professor, naturalist, alchemist and traveller?

There are none anywhere, because he was persecuted for heresy, and his works were publicly burnt in 1573.

Very good! Excellent!

Now it is clear. That's why he had to use a complicated code to bury the secret--

What!

Ummm... I mean... no secret. I was only supposing a case.

Well, I hope you will not leave our island until you have seen its wealth of minerals. Mount Sneffels, for example...

...is a long extinct volcano, and its crater has been rarely visited.

That is a delightful idea. We will climb to the summit of Sneffels and, if possible, descend into its crater.

I shall arrange a guide.

The man sent to guide us was Hans Bjelke – a calm and silent individual.

He appeared to possess very great strength. He did not seem lazy, but his appearance suggested tranquillity.

Since he worked as an eiderdown hunter, he knew the area well.

Four horses were prepared for us; two to carry the baggage, and two to bear the weight of myself and my uncle.

A great fellow, but completely unaware of the marvellous part he has to play in the future.

Hans declared that nothing would ever make him climb on the back of an animal.

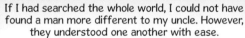

If I had searched the whole world, I could not have found a man more different to my uncle. However, they understood one another with ease.

So he is to go with us as far as--

As far as the centre of the Earth, Henry.

There were still forty-eight hours to go before we set out. And, to my great regret, the whole time was taken up in making preparations for our journey.

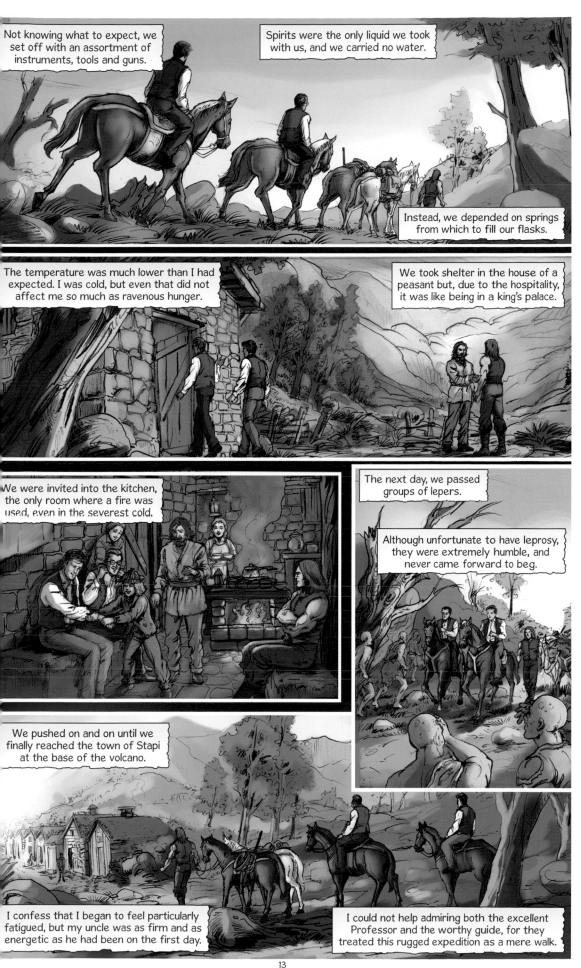

This was the last stop on our journey before reaching Sneffels. Hans had guided us with reliability and intelligence.

In Stapi, he hired the services of three men to take care of the horses which would transport our belongings.

The priests here received a pittance from the Danish government.

The next day, 23rd June, we left Stapi behind us.

There was no proof that Sneffels was extinct. Who could assure us that an eruption was not brewing at that very moment?

We stayed at the Rector's house, in a small and uncomfortable cabin, and he fleeced us.

If he suddenly wakes, what is to become of us?

I was thinking of that.

Nothing would be more foolish than to act without due care.

It is now 600 years since Sneffels last spoke and, though reduced to a state of utter silence, he may speak again.

I have closely examined this region; I have studied the soil, my dear Henry, and there will be no eruption.

You doubt my word? Well, follow me.

I obeyed without question.

14

We were soon in open country, which was covered with volcanic deposits. I could see many spouts of steam rising in the air. They came from hot water fountains, and indicated the volcanic activity of the soil.

You see all this steam, Henry?

Yes.

If an eruption was approaching, these ...ts would increase their activity, and would then disappear altogether during the eruption itself.

But--

My uncle had completely defeated me with his scientific arguments. Nevertheless, I still had one hope.

Enough, my boy.

If the steam remains in its normal state, we can be sure that there is no fear of an immediate eruption.

I hoped that once we reached the bottom of the crater, there would be no tunnels and it would be impossible to descend any deeper.

I was quite reassured about the fate of our enterprise, and therefore continued, like a brave soldier, towards the assault of old Sneffels.

Occasionally, Hans would stop to pile up lumps of rock into small heaps, to prevent us getting lost on our return. He had no idea of the journey we were about to undertake.

My uncle stuck as close to me as possible and never lost sight of me. On many occasions his arm supplied me with firm and solid support.

He was strong, athletic and seemed oblivious to fatigue.

The Professor could tell that my legs had stopped working, and that I was utterly exhausted.

I think we should stop and rest.

He called Hans to his side, but he just shook his head.

Ofvanfor!

Come on. We must go higher.

He then turned to Hans, and asked him to give a reason why we must continue.

Mistour.

Ja, mistour!

Mistour? Uncle, what does that word mean?

They have spotted something. We must climb higher to see.

Hastigt! Hastigt!

I knew no Danish, but I understood that his gestures were meant to make us move quicker.

Oh my!

There was a colossal mass of pulverised pumice stone, sand and dust rising to the heavens.

SSHHFOOSH

This extraordinary phenomenon happens when the wind shakes the glaciers and sweeps over the arid plains. In Icelandic it is called mistour.

The wind was driving it directly towards us. Only the precaution and knowledge of our guide ensured our dislocated bodies, and our crushed and broken limbs, were not carried away with the wind, like dust from some unknown meteor.

We pushed onwards despite our fatigue.

I had never felt such misery and exhaustion in my life. I was ready to faint from hunger and cold.

At last, we reached the summit of Mount Sneffels. Although I was tired, I paused to enjoy the spectacle of the Sun's pale rays being cast upon the mountain.

Hurry, Henry! Look! Down here.

Do you still doubt?

We were both utterly amazed. But his amazement soon turned to the wildest joy.

And so, on the eastern side of the huge block of stone, we found some characters. They were half eaten away by the corrosive action of time, but they spelt out a name.

Arne Saknussemm!

It was impossible for me to say anything. The evidence was unanswerable, overwhelming.

The next morning, a grey, cloudy, heavy sky hung over the summit of the volcano. I did not notice it so much from the sky itself, as from my uncle's anger.

It was already 25th June. If the skies would just remain densely clouded for six more days, we would have to put off our voyage of discovery for another year.

And the following year there would certainly be one less person in the party. I had already had enough of the mad enterprise.

The parchment said the shadow of that peak would lead us to the right path at the end of June.

We waited day...

...after day...

...after day.

On Sunday 28th, with a sudden change of wind and a new Moon, there came a change of weather. And the Sun poured its beaming rays down upon us.

There it is! Now for the centre of the Earth.

To my uncle's delight, the shadow of Scartaris was marked and clear, and moved slowly with the radiant start of day.

It measured about 100 feet in diameter, which made it about 300 in circumference. I looked down, my hair stood on end, my teeth chattered and my limbs trembled.

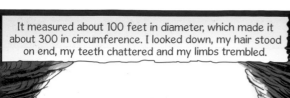

I seemed to lose my centre of gravity, and my head began to whirl, like that of a drunken man.

AAH!

There is nothing more powerful than the attraction towards an abyss.

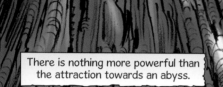

I was about to fall headfirst into the gaping well, when I was pulled back by a firm and powerful hand.

We have to carry everything ourselves from now on.

Let's split the provisions three ways.

Everyone ready?

Hans accepted the enterprise with such calmness, paying no attention to the possible dangers, that I blushed at the idea of being less brave than him.

One by one, we made the descent.

The water ran out completely by the end of the first day's return journey.

Our provision of liquids was reduced to our supply of gin. But this infernal liquor burnt the throat, and I could not even bear the sight of it.

The temperature was stifling. I was paralysed with fatigue and more than once I nearly collapsed.

Drink, my poor boy.

We all stopped, and the worthy Icelander and my excellent uncle did their best to console and comfort me.

GLUG GLUG GLUG

It is the very last. I had kept it as a precious treasure at the bottom of my flask.

This did not quench my thirst, but I had nevertheless partially recovered my strength.

We have no water; we must go back.

Uncle?

I have started this expedition, and I will carry it out to the end or I will not return.

Take Hans with you; leave me to myself.

I could see that my uncle was struggling with the extreme fatigues of our journey, and the awful torture generated by the absence of water.

We must go back!

We must drag him with us. Do you hear me? Do you understand?

Our guide was looking on with utter calmness and indifference. He never moved a muscle, but remained motionless. He just gently shook his head and pointed to my uncle.

Be calm, Henry! I ask you for one more day.

In one more day, if we have not found the water that we want, I swear to you we will return to the surface of the Earth.

Despite my irritation and despair, I knew how difficult it was for my uncle to say this. Under the circumstances, what could I do but agree?

The direction of our march was, in general, towards the southwest. That day and the next, we did a considerable amount of horizontal travelling.

On 10th July, a horrible well opened under our feet and our descent then began.

Fifty leagues from Mount Sneffels.

Fifty leagues horizontally from where we started.

But that would put us--

If your calculations are correct, we are no longer under Iceland.

We are under the open sea!

Yes, there is no doubt that the old Ocean flows over our heads!

ICELAND

But what can be more natural! Do you not know that near to Newcastle there are coal mines which work far out under the sea?

By 15th July, we were actually seven leagues below the surface of the Earth, and fifty leagues from the mountain of Sneffels.

SWISH SWASH

How did it matter if the mountains of Iceland, or the mighty Atlantic Ocean were above our heads? Either way, we were reliant on the solidity of the granite roof above us.

29

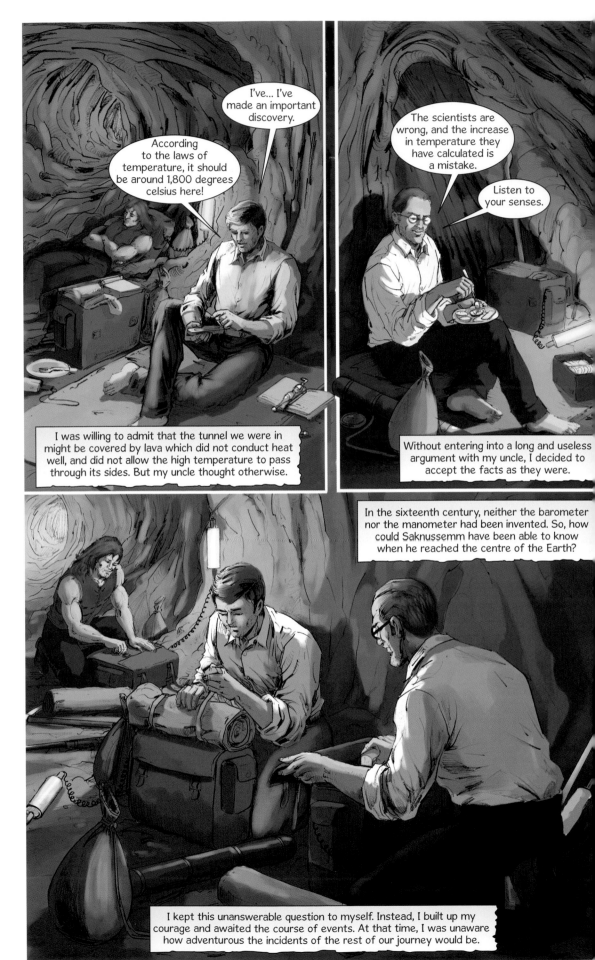

No words could describe my despair. I was buried alive, with no option but to die a slow and horrible death from hunger and thirst.

I crawled around, feeling the dry and arid rock. I had never felt anything so dry.

How had I lost the course of the flowing stream? Regardless of how, it explained the strange silence which prevailed.

Lost! LOST! LOST!

There were absolutely no clues or landmarks.

The 100 miles of the crust of the Earth weighed upon my shoulders like the globe on the shoulders of Atlas. I felt myself crushed by this awful weight.

I was in a position that would drive the sanest man to madness!

Knowing that I was utterly powerless to do anything to save myself, I knelt and asked for assistance from Heaven.

With a strange sense of despair, I watched the light of my lamp getting less and less.

The absolute obscurity made me blind in every sense

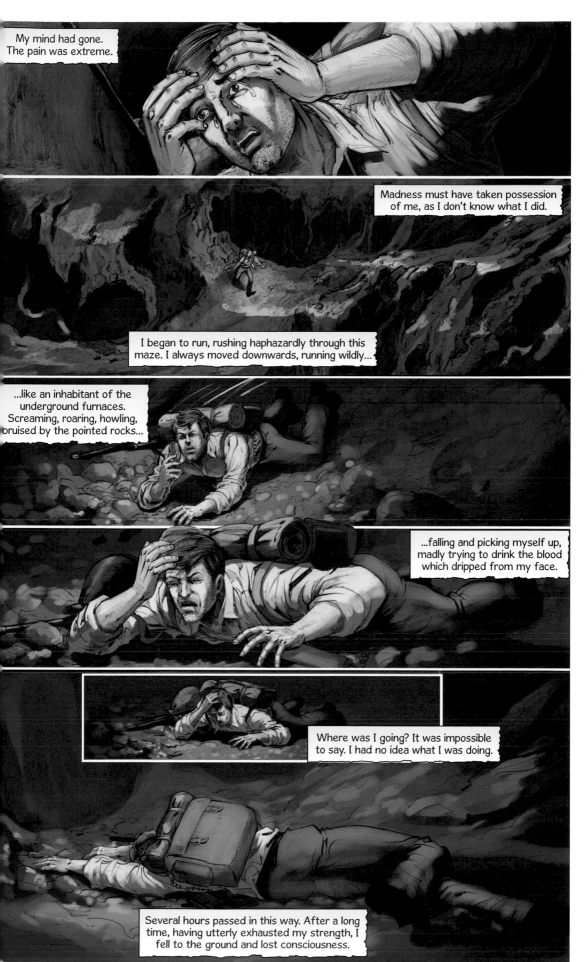

When I came back to my senses, my face was wet, but I soon realised this was due to tears. How long my state of insensibility lasted, it is impossible for me to say.

All of a sudden, a violent sound, like the rumbling of thunder, reached my ears. I could clearly hear voices, getting lost in the distant depths of the gulf.

Again I listened carefully. With my ear against the wall, I managed to catch the faintest echo of a sound.

THIS IS...
THIS IS...
THIS IS...
THIS IS...
THIS IS...
THIS IS...

Uncle Hardwigg!

I thought that I could hear vague and distant voices. I started shaking with excitement and hope!

Henry, my boy? Where are you?

Lost! The lamp is out. The stream disappeared.

Keep your courage, Henry. We will find you.

It took twenty seconds for your voice to reach us.

At about 1,000 feet per second, we're a league and a half away.

This wonderful and surprising conversation, which took place through the vast maze of tunnels, ended with words of hope.

I uttered one more prayer to Heaven, and gave thanks. God had led me to the only place where the voices of my friends could reach me.

And, as my eyes adjusted to the light, I saw a vast, limitless expanse of water. A lake, if not an ocean, lay before us, until it was lost in the distance.

The vapours above us lit up the sky like the Sun. But, it was not like the Sun as it gave off no heat.

On all sides were headlands and enormous cliffs, worn down by the eternal breaking of the waves!

Do you feel strong enough to explore?

The sea? The sea!

Yes, the Central Sea. No future navigator will be able to deny that I discovered it. And, therefore, I have the right to give it this name.

It was actually an ocean, with the characteristics of an inland sea. It was horribly wild – so rigid, cold and savage.

I wondered whether I was awake; whether I was dreaming; whether my brain was affected by imaginary noises. But eyes and ears cannot be so completely deceived.

The unexpected spectacle restored some colour to my pale cheeks. I actually seemed to be getting better because of this discovery.

As my uncle led me, my attention was drawn to an astonishing sight.

It is a forest. A forest of...

This forest consisted of straight trunks with tufted tops, shaped like parasols. When we reached the forest, and stood beneath the trees, my surprise gave way to admiration.

I was simply in the presence of a very ordinary product of the Earth, but of gigantic proportions.

...mushrooms. Look around you! Botanists have never seen anything like this.

These are plants from the prehistoric era. And...

...bones... of a mastodon! More than 100 miles below the surface of the Earth?

Why not? At one time the crust of the Earth was elastic.

It is likely that large amounts of soil slid into huge chasms like this, allowing life to exist.

What now? Are you thinking of returning to the surface?

Return! No, indeed not!

I looked around, examining every point of the horizon with care, but nothing living appeared to exist on these deserted shores.

The tide is now at its highest point.

What! Did you say the tide, Uncle?

Do you mean that the influence of the Sun and Moon is felt here too?

Why not? Why should this underground sea be exempt from the rules of the Universe?

We will travel to the other end of this sea and continue our journey. I suspect, on the opposite shores, we shall find new passages.

And how far do you think this sea extends?

Thirty or forty leagues. We have no time to lose, and shall set sail tomorrow.

What! You want us to launch out upon an unknown sea. Where will the boat take us?

My dear Henry, if you would listen instead of talking so much, you would hear the sound of a hammer. Hans has been at work for many hours.

Well, my dear boy, it is not exactly what you would call a boat. For the time being, we must be content with a good and solid raft.

A raft! But down here it's just as impossible to build a raft as a boat.

The raft was made from beams of a very peculiar wood, and a great number of limbs, joints and boughs lay about. There was enough wood to construct a fleet of ships.

39

40

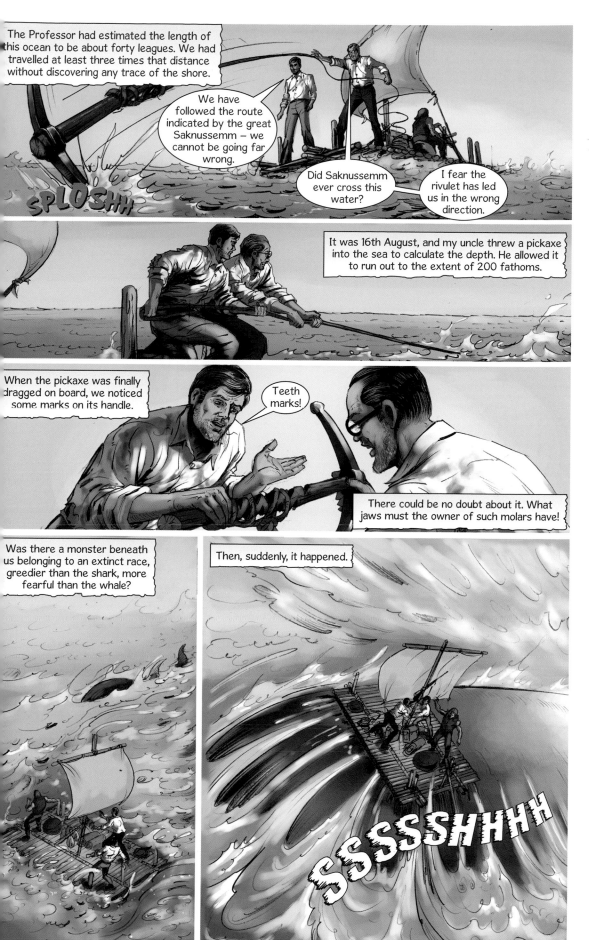

The Professor had estimated the length of this ocean to be about forty leagues. We had travelled at least three times that distance without discovering any trace of the shore.

We have followed the route indicated by the great Saknussemm – we cannot be going far wrong.

Did Saknussemm ever cross this water?

I fear the rivulet has led us in the wrong direction.

SPLOSHH

It was 16th August, and my uncle threw a pickaxe into the sea to calculate the depth. He allowed it to run out to the extent of 200 fathoms.

When the pickaxe was finally dragged on board, we noticed some marks on its handle.

Teeth marks!

There could be no doubt about it. What jaws must the owner of such molars have!

Was there a monster beneath us belonging to an extinct race, greedier than the shark, more fearful than the whale?

Then, suddenly, it happened.

SSSSHHHH

41

The raft was lifted up on a watery mountain and then dropped down again, at a distance of twenty fathoms.

What is it?

A colossal monster! How many are there?

RRRRRAARGH

We stood still – surprised, astonished, terror-stricken at the sight of this group of fearful marine monsters, more hideous in reality than in my wildest dreams.

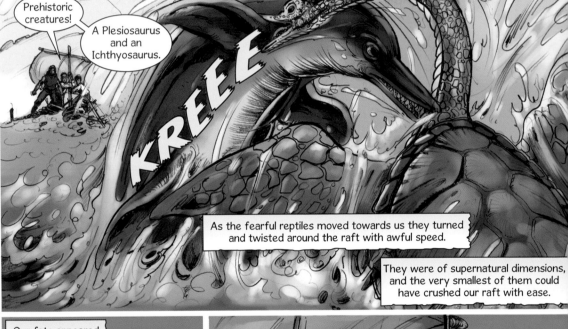

Prehistoric creatures!

A Plesiosaurus and an Ichthyosaurus.

KREEE

As the fearful reptiles moved towards us they turned and twisted around the raft with awful speed.

They were of supernatural dimensions, and the very smallest of them could have crushed our raft with ease.

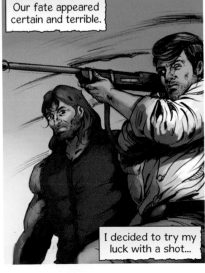

Our fate appeared certain and terrible.

I decided to try my luck with a shot...

...but fortunatel Hans stopped m

We were not their targets.

We could distinctly see the two monsters engaged in deadly conflict.

The warriors moved closer and then further away from our raft. Those huge creatures attacked each other with the greatest animosity.

They raised mountains of water which rocked our raft perilously. On many occasions we nearly capsized.

The struggle continued ferociously for two hours. We remained ready to fire. Suddenly, the creatures disappeared below, leaving a whirlpool in the water.

The monster's long neck shot up and dropped down, coiled and uncoiled, lashed the waters like a gigantic whip and writhed like a worm, until it stopped moving altogether.

Der nere.*

What! Another sea beast?

Yes, yes, there it is.

On 20th August, the horizon was perfectly calm, clear and free from all haze.

Having christened the volcanic island in my name, we moved on, leaving it behind us.

No, an island with a boiling geyser, or water spout, like those common in Iceland. Jets like this are an amazing wonder.

I made some observations to calculate the distance we had covered. Since we had left Port Gretchen, we had travelled 270 leagues – more than 800 miles – on this great inland sea.

There's a storm coming on.

We were, therefore, 620 leagues from Iceland and right under England.

*There.

By ten o'clock the next morning, the storm had become stronger and more extreme.

We should take in the sail.

No, no, a hundred times, no. Let the wind do its worst; let the storm force us where it wants. Even if our raft gets dashed into a thousand pieces we must keep the sail up.

The horizon changed suddenly and violently. It raged from every point of the compass. It roared; it yelled; it shrieked with joy as if demons were being let loose.

44

We had travelled 200 leagues since we left the neighbourhood of Henry's Island.

The lightning didn't stop flashing for a single moment. It plunged its forked streaks in every direction.

BADABOOM

For three days we had not been able to hear each other speak. Our mouths opened, our lips moved, but not a word could be heard. We could not even make ourselves heard by placing our mouths to each other's ears.

One bolt of lightning was like a ball of fire. It magnetised every iron object on board. Even the nails in our boots – I couldn't move my foot at all.

BDAAM

The electricity coursed through us. It jolted our bodies, and made us feel like we were on fire.

Oh, what intense, stupendous light!

...if my body was not torn by the sharp edges of the rocks, it was because the powerful arm of Hans came to my rescue.

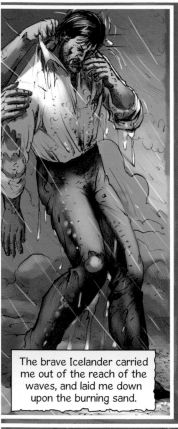

The brave Icelander carried me out of the reach of the waves, and laid me down upon the burning sand.

We have got to the end of that endless sea.

Allow me to ask you one question, Uncle.

Certainly, Henry. Ask a dozen if you like.

One will do. How about returning?

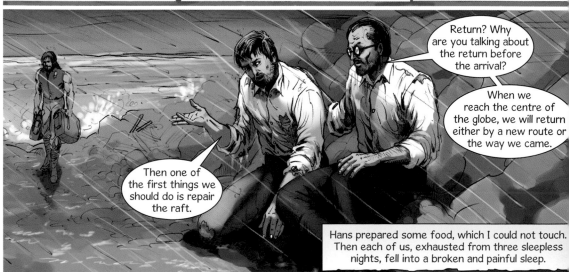

Return? Why are you talking about the return before the arrival?

When we reach the centre of the globe, we will return either by a new route or the way we came.

Then one of the first things we should do is repair the raft.

Hans prepared some food, which I could not touch. Then each of us, exhausted from three sleepless nights, fell into a broken and painful sleep.

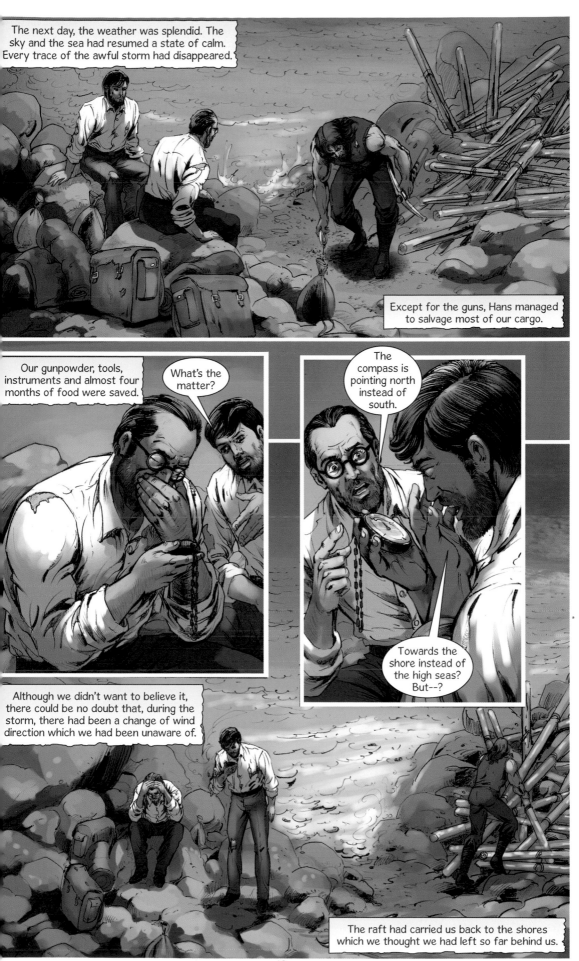

The next day, the weather was splendid. The sky and the sea had resumed a state of calm. Every trace of the awful storm had disappeared.

Except for the guns, Hans managed to salvage most of our cargo.

Our gunpowder, tools, instruments and almost four months of food were saved.

What's the matter?

The compass is pointing north instead of south.

Towards the shore instead of the high seas? But--?

Although we didn't want to believe it, there could be no doubt that, during the storm, there had been a change of wind direction which we had been unaware of.

The raft had carried us back to the shores which we thought we had left so far behind us.

49

Will fate play tricks upon me? Will the elements plot against me? I will not give up!

It is useless to struggle against the impossible. Listen to reason, Uncle.

Although we had arrived back at the northern shore, we had landed at a very different spot from where we started.

I will never give up!

The raft will be repaired by tomorrow. Let's examine the coast till then.

It would be impossible for me to explain the utter astonishment, disbelief and rage that overcame the Professor on making this extraordinary discovery.

And leaving Hans to his important operation, we started on our expedition.

We advanced with great difficulty, until a large field of bones appeared suddenly before our eyes. It looked like an immense cemetery.

Henry, my boy!

A human head!

We stood amongst an endless and wondrously rich collection of prehistoric monsters.

Imagine an enthusiastic book lover being transported back in time to the famous library of Alexandria!

Before our departure, a human bone had been discovered fourteen feet below the surface of the Earth. It was the first fossil of its kind that had ever been found. Near to these human remains were some stone tools.

The authenticity of a human fossil from two million years ago seemed to have been proven beyond doubt. Even the sceptics agreed.

Did man exist alongside, or even before, beasts like mastodons?

And here, deep inside the Earth, was undeniable proof.

Human and animal remains of the Quaternary period buried together.

But had they been buried far beneath the soil by the shifting earth...

...or had they lived here?

We had already seen live fish and marine monsters.

But were there also underground men wandering about the deserted shores of this wondrous sea?

For another half hour, we walked across a floor of bones. We pushed on, motivated by our curiosity. What other marvels did this place contain?

The brightness of the light enabled us to see the smallest objects in the distant trees. We thought we could see gigantic animals moving about...

Come on! Forward! Forward!

Come! Come along, my boy. Let us take a closer look.

...a whole herd of mastodons – not fossils, but living. I could hear the sounds of the mighty tusks of these enormous elephants uprooting huge trees!

No! We have no weapons.

No human being can survive the anger of these monsters.

You are wrong, Henry. Look down there!

It looks like a human being – a being like ourselves – a man!

I could not believe my eyes.

Impossible!

Not far away, walking past the trunk of an enormous tree, was a human being – a product of this underground region.

He was of a great height. His head, as big as the head of a buffalo, was covered in a mane of matted hair. It was like a mane belonging to a prehistoric elephant.

THUMP
THUMP

We remained still, speechless with surprise.

Maybe. But very real.

He might have seen us at any minute, so we had no choice but to run.

Come on!

I dragged my uncle along and, for the first time, he didn't try to stop me.

Well, this is strange. It can't belong to Hans.

And the steel – it can't be from the stone age or the bronze period.

Correct, Henry. This weapon is the type of dagger worn by gentlemen in their belts during the sixteenth century.

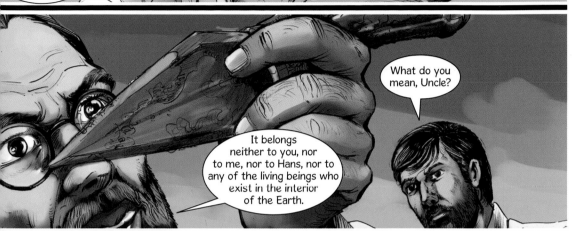

What do you mean, Uncle?

It belongs neither to you, nor to me, nor to Hans, nor to any of the living beings who exist in the interior of the Earth.

It did, however, belong to the man who has engraved his name somewhere with it. That man wanted to mark the way to the centre of the Earth again. Let us look around.

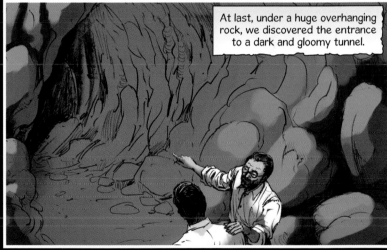

At last, under a huge overhanging rock, we discovered the entrance to a dark and gloomy tunnel.

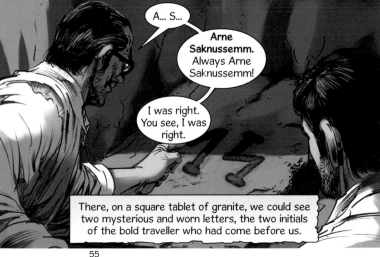

A... S...

Arne Saknussemm. Always Arne Saknussemm!

I was right. You see, I was right.

We walked along the wall of rock, examining even the smallest cracks, hoping to find the shaft or tunnel we were looking for.

There, on a square tablet of granite, we could see two mysterious and worn letters, the two initials of the bold traveller who had come before us.

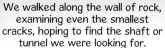

It was 27th August and nothing was impossible now.

Wonderful and glorious genius. We shall name this Cape Saknussemm.

Let us go back to Hans, and bring the raft here.

On returning to our patient guide, we found he had prepared everything for an immediate departure.

So, we rafted back to the entrance of the tunnel we had found.

I was in a state of excitement and enthusiasm.

The opening was almost circular. Inside, our progress was stopped by an enormous block of granite rock.

We looked to the right and the left, and examined above and below it. But it was in vain, as there was no sign of any other passage or tunnel.

Was Arne Saknussemm stopped by this stone barrier?

It has been shaken down by some disturbance. Let us go to work with the pickaxe.

That won't work, but we can use the gunpowder.

To work, Hans, to work!

The Icelander went back to the raft, and soon returned with a huge crowbar. With this he began to dig a hole in the rock to use as a mine.

We needed to make a space large enough to hold fifty pounds of exploding gun cotton – an explosive which is much more powerful than ordinary gunpowder.

57

The rocks were drawn aside like a curtain.

RUMMMBBBLE

The explosion caused a kind of earthquake and the soil was broken by cracks and vents.

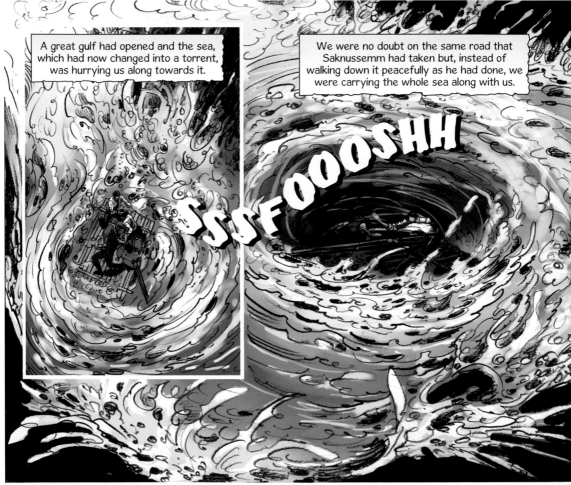

A great gulf had opened and the sea, which had now changed into a torrent, was hurrying us along towards it.

We were no doubt on the same road that Saknussemm had taken but, instead of walking down it peacefully as he had done, we were carrying the whole sea along with us.

SSSFOOOOSHH

Judging by the passing rocks, we were travelling at least 100 miles an hour.

Most of our cargo was gone – not a pickaxe, or crowbar, or hammer remained.

And worst of all, there was only enough food for a day!

This discovery meant a certain and horrible death.

The light went out, and there was a rush of air in the darkness.

The descent became steeper. I believe we had stopped sliding, and were now falling.

Suddenly, I felt a shock. The raft had not struck anything, but its progress had suddenly been stopped. A waterspout, a column of water, hit us.

I felt like I was being drowned.

But, in a few seconds, I was able to breathe again, and I inhaled the air with the full strength of my lungs.

I noticed that my uncle and Hans were holding me tight by the arms, and then we were carried away again.

FWISH

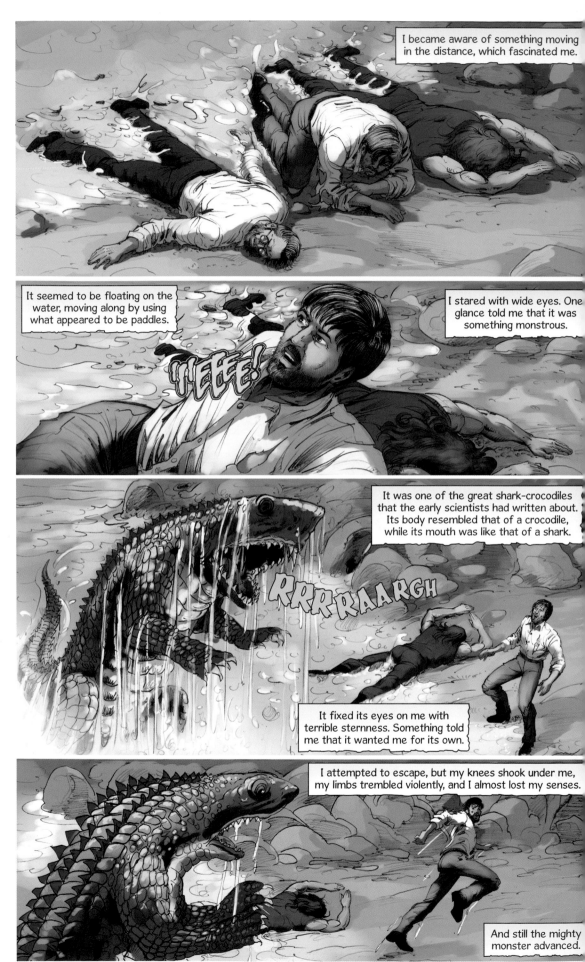

I became aware of something moving in the distance, which fascinated me.

It seemed to be floating on the water, moving along by using what appeared to be paddles.

I stared with wide eyes. One glance told me that it was something monstrous.

WEEE!

It was one of the great shark-crocodiles that the early scientists had written about. Its body resembled that of a crocodile, while its mouth was like that of a shark.

RRRRAARGH

It fixed its eyes on me with terrible sternness. Something told me that it wanted me for its own.

I attempted to escape, but my knees shook under me, my limbs trembled violently, and I almost lost my senses.

And still the mighty monster advanced.

...awoke from my nightmare.

Yes... it was all a dream. I was still on the raft with my uncle and Hans.

I did not feel relieved straight away, as the nightmare had numbed my senses. I listened carefully, but everything was as still as death. All I comprehended was silence.

Perfect peace came after the roaring of the waters. The awful reverberations of earlier had stopped.

Look. We're going up, higher and higher.

While there is life, there is hope.

We can eat, which will give us the strength to face victory or death.

We were mounting at a speed of about ten miles an hour.

Prolonged hunger causes temporary madness. The brain cannot work without food, and crazy ideas fill the mind.

When this piece of meat is finished, there will be no food left. What hope will we have then?

None, my dear Henry, none. But will it do you any good just to look at it?

Do you mean to tell me that you... that you have not lost all hope?

Certainly not.

You mean to tell me, Uncle, that we will get out of this underground shaft?

While there is life, there is hope. As long as a man's heart beats, I don't think he should despair.

Well, what do you intend to do?

Eat what remains of the food we have in our hands. It could be our last meal, but at least we will be men once again and not exhausted skeletons.

True. Let us take our fill.

Hans swallowed every mouthful as if everything was normal. His upbringing had probably prepared him for many sufferings.

Schiedam*.

*Gin.

We drank. My uncle and I will admit to our dying day that the gin gave us the strength to exist until the last bitter moment.

That precious bottle was only half full but, under the circumstances, it was like nectar.

By the time we had consumed our last ounce of food, it was five o'clock in the morning!

My thoughts were made up of memories of the world above - the surface of the Earth which I should never have left.

As we rose higher, the temperature increased dramatically, and I began to feel like I was being bathed in a hot and fiery atmosphere.

The wall is burning hot.

And the water is scalding.

URRGL URRGL URRGL

I had never felt anything like it before.

Can't you feel the heat and see the rocks cracking? Can't you see how the water is boiling? And how the dense vapours and steam are growing thicker with every minute?

BDAAM

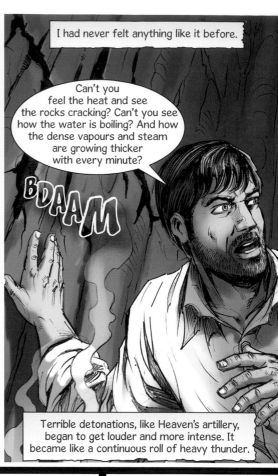

Terrible detonations, like Heaven's artillery, began to get louder and more intense. It became like a continuous roll of heavy thunder.

All of these signs suggest an awful earthquake!

My uncle made no reply except for a gesture of despair.

Then something close to the truth struck his mind.

It's not an earthquake! I am expecting something far more important.

I strained my brain to the limits – what did he mean?

An eruption!

It is the most fortunate thing that could happen to us.

Fortunate! We are about to be ejected in a whirlwind of flames.

The most fortunate thing! Had my uncle actually gone mad? What did he mean by these words? How could he maintain this terrible calm, this solemn smile?

It is impossible for me describe the strange, wild thoughts which ran through my mind following this extraordinary announcement.

It is our only chance to reach the surface of the Earth.

GLUG GLUG

My uncle was right. And, when he looked me calmly in the eye and spoke of being thrown back to Earth through the gaping crater of a volcano, I felt that he had never appeared so bold and so convinced before.

The whole night we continued rising higher. The fearful noise increased and I was ready to suffocate. I seriously believed that my last hour was approaching.

RRMMMBL

In such circumstances, you do not choose your own thoughts. They overcome you.

We were being pushed upwards by eruptive matter. Under the raft there was a mass of boiling water, lava and rocks. On reaching the summit, these would be dispersed in every direction.

There was no longer any doubt that we were inside the chimney of a volcano. But, on this occasion, instead of Sneffels, an old and extinct volcano, we were inside a mountain of fire in full activity.

I could think of nothing more terrible! And then it happened.

BOOM

A storm of wind suddenly roused up the interior fires of the Earth. It was a hot, incandescent blast!

I felt the hand of Hans gripping me firmly. With the other arm he supported my uncle. I was not seriously hurt, but I was shaken, and bruised and battered all over.

Hans had, once again, saved me from death.

I expected to see a mountain covered by snow, and thought we would be surrounded by glaciers in the middle of the extreme northern regions.

But, contrary to my expectations, we were on the slope of a mountain burnt by the rays of the Sun. And we were literally being baked by it.

The radiant Sun, which we had not seen for two months, was good enough to provide us with light and warmth – a light and warmth which we didn't really require.

Where can we be? Are we back in Iceland?

It does not look like Iceland.

Whatever this mountain is, it's rather warm. Let us walk down the mountain and discover where we really are.

According to the compass we have always been going northwards.

We are in Asia. We are on the coast of India. We are in the great Malay islands. We are in the centre of Oceania. We are at the other end of Europe!

The plain truth was that there was no explanation possible.

A beautiful country spread out before us. While we were enjoying the delights of the place we found ourselves in, a little child appeared.

The little fellow was poorly dressed, weak and suffering, and was alarmed by our appearance.

Ah! Here is an inhabitant of this land!

My uncle tried talking in German and French and Italian.

What is the name of this mountain, my friend?

The child shook his head and made no reply. I became puzzled.

<Come si noma questa isola?> What is the name of this island?

Stromboli.

He spoke another dialect of the Italian language.

Stromboli! We were in the centre of the Mediterranean. And those blue mountains, which rose towards the rising Sun, were the mountains of Calabria.

Stromboli! Stromboli!

What a journey — what a marvellous and extraordinary journey! We had entered the Earth by one volcano and had come out by another.

And this volcano was situated more than 1,200 leagues from Sneffels.

We reached Hamburg on 9th October. Later, I checked our compass and discovered that the poles had changed!

Gretchen was so happy to see me return.

Now that you really are a hero, Henry, there is no reason why you should ever leave me again.

Hans left Hamburg. The man to whom we owed so much would not allow us to repay our deep debt of gratitude.

He became nostalgic and longed to return to his Icelandic home.

We were deeply attached to our brave eider duck hunter. He will never be forgotten by those whose lives he saved, and I hope to see him again one day.

My uncle became a great man, and I, the nephew of a great man. Hamburg gave a festival in our honour.

Our journey into the interior of the Earth created an enormous sensation throughout the civilised world.

My uncle enjoyed all the glory and honour.

And with Gretchen as my wife...

...I became the happiest of ordinary mortals.

CAMPFIRE™

About Us

It is night-time in the forest. The sky is black, studded with countless stars. A campfire is crackling, and the storytelling has begun. Stories about love and wisdom, conflict and power, dreams and identity, courage and adventure, survival against all odds, and hope against all hope – they have all come to the fore in a stream of words, gestures, song and dance. The warm, cheerful radiance of the campfire has awoken the storyteller in all those present. Even the trees and the earth and the animals of the forest seem to have fallen silent, captivated, bewitched.

Inspired by this enduring relationship between a campfire and the stories it evokes, we began publishing under the Campfire imprint in 2008, with the vision of creating graphic novels of the finest quality to entertain and educate our readers. Our writers, editors, artists and colourists share a deep passion for good stories and the art of storytelling, so our books are well researched, beautifully illustrated and wonderfully written to create a most enjoyable reading experience.

Our graphic novels are presently being published in four exciting categories. The *Classics* category showcases popular and timeless literature, which has been faithfully adapted for today's readers. While these adaptations retain the flavour of the era, they encourage our readers to delve into the literary world with the aid of authentic graphics and simplified language. Titles in the *Originals* category feature imaginative new characters and intriguing plots, and will be highly anticipated and appreciated by lovers of fiction. Our *Mythology* titles tap into the vast library of epics, myths, and legends from India and abroad, not just presenting tales from time immemorial, but also addressing their modern-day relevance. And our *Biography* titles explore the life and times of eminent personalities from around the world, in a manner that is both inspirational and personal.

Crafted by a new generation of talented artists and writers, all our graphic novels boast cutting-edge artwork, an engaging narrative, and have universal and lasting appeal.

Whether you are an avid reader or an occasional one, we hope you will gather around our campfire and let us draw you into our fascinating world of storytelling.

WHAT ARE VOLCANOES?

A volcano is an opening in the crust of the Earth through which molten lava, various gases and ash are released.

Below the surface of the Earth, there is often an accumulation of gas-rich magma (molten underground rock). This collects due to the partial melting of the crust and the mantle which is, in turn, caused by high temperatures far below the ground. Volcanoes are vents, cracks, or weak places in the Earth's surface through which lava, steam, ashes, etc., are expelled, either continuously or at irregular intervals. When the molten rock reaches the Earth's surface through the fissure, it becomes lava. Ash is also released with lava, often to devastating effect. Gas clouds, which are hot and ash-laden, can scorch vegetation and kill animals and people by suffocating them.

The large magma chamber uses the volcano, as a vent, to escape to the surface. The magma travels through the volcano using a conduit (pipe). When the magma erupts from the vent, it shatters layers of rock into small particles which results in ash dispersal. Solidified lava, ashes and cinder form the cone. Layers of lava alternate with layers of ash to make the steep-sided cone higher and higher.

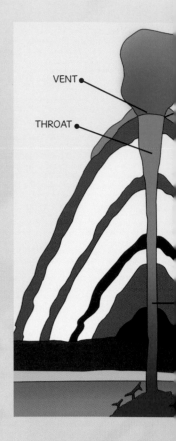

VENT

THROAT

Which is the most active volcano in the world?

Kilauea, which forms a part of the Hawaiian Islands in the United States is said to be the world's most active volcano. The slopes of this volcanic mass are joined with Mauna Loa another active volcano, on two sides. In 1790, an eruption from the volcano killed many members of the Hawaiian army. One of its most destructive eruptions occurred in 1955 and the volcano continues to spew lava at an alarming rate to this day.

What is the Hawaii Volcanoes National Park?

It is an area made up of volcanoes and volcanic matter along the southeast shore of the Hawaiian Islands. The two famous active volcanoes – Mauna Loa and Kilauea – are located in this region. The Kau Desert, the Mauna Loa Trail, a tree-fern forest and a museum are all part of the Park.

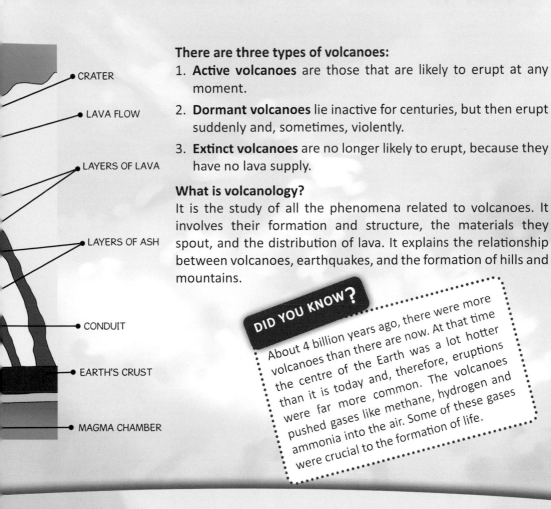

CRATER

LAVA FLOW

LAYERS OF LAVA

LAYERS OF ASH

CONDUIT

EARTH'S CRUST

MAGMA CHAMBER

There are three types of volcanoes:

1. **Active volcanoes** are those that are likely to erupt at any moment.
2. **Dormant volcanoes** lie inactive for centuries, but then erupt suddenly and, sometimes, violently.
3. **Extinct volcanoes** are no longer likely to erupt, because they have no lava supply.

What is volcanology?

It is the study of all the phenomena related to volcanoes. It involves their formation and structure, the materials they spout, and the distribution of lava. It explains the relationship between volcanoes, earthquakes, and the formation of hills and mountains.

DID YOU KNOW?

About 4 billion years ago, there were more volcanoes than there are now. At that time the centre of the Earth was a lot hotter than it is today and, therefore, eruptions were far more common. The volcanoes pushed gases like methane, hydrogen and ammonia into the air. Some of these gases were crucial to the formation of life.

HAVE YOU EVER HEARD OF THE ANCIENT ITALIAN CITY CALLED POMPEII?

Pompeii was a thriving city that was destroyed when a volcano named Mount Vesuvius erupted. It killed many of the city's inhabitants and left behind a perfectly preserved example of ancient life in the Mediterranean.

The catastrophe occurred in 79 AD in the towns of Pompeii and Herculaneum. The rumbling volcano completely buried both towns with ash and pumice. The towns sank about three metres under boiling lava and other volcanic matter. Eye witness reports in the form of letters document this fact. Many were buried under the flood of lava as they tried to shield their homes and families, while others suffocated to death.

Domenico Fontana, an architect, first discovered the remains of Pompeii in the sixteenth century. In 1951, more extensive excavation began under the supervision of Amedeo Maiuri. The most significant architectural structure discovered was a large basilica. The excavations provide an insight into the social, political, religious, and even personal life of the people.

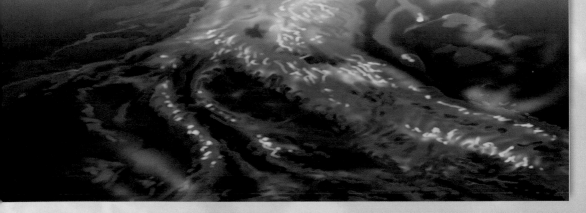

Available now

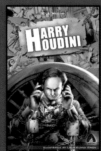

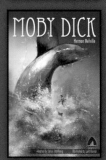